TORONTO RAPTORS

ALL-TIME GREATS

BY BRENDAN FLYNN

Book design by Jake Slavik
Cover design by Jake Slavik

Photographs ©: Frank Gunn/The Canadian Press/AP Images, cover (top), 1 (top); Mark Lennihan/AP Images, cover (bottom), 1 (bottom); Lisa Blumenfeld/Getty Images Sport/Getty Images, 4, 9; Bob Rosato/Sports Illustrated/Set Number: X65301 TK2/Getty Images, 6; Jeff Gross/Getty Images Sport/Getty Images, 10; Vaughn Ridley/Getty Images Sport/Getty Images, 13; Elsa/Getty Images Sport/Getty Images, 14; Ezra Shaw/Getty Images Sport/Getty Images, 16; Greg Nelson/Sports Illustrated/Set Number: X162667 TK1/Getty Images, 19; Kyle Terada/Getty Images Sport/Getty Images, 20; Red Line Editorial, 22

Press Box Books, an imprint of Press Room Editions.

ISBN
978-1-63494-161-7 (library bound)
978-1-63494-174-7 (paperback)
978-1-63494-187-7 (epub)
978-1-63494-200-3 (hosted ebook)

Library of Congress Control Number: 2019951066

Distributed by North Star Editions, Inc.
2297 Waters Drive
Mendota Heights, MN 55120
www.northstareditions.com

Printed in the United States of America
012020

ABOUT THE AUTHOR

Brendan Flynn is a San Francisco resident and an author of numerous children's books. In addition to writing about sports, Flynn also enjoys competing in triathlons, Scrabble tournaments, and chili cook-offs.

TABLE OF CONTENTS

CARTER
15
DIRECTV
Clippers
RAPTORS
4

CHAPTER 1

EXPANSION ERA

The Toronto Raptors are one of the NBA's newest teams. They began as an expansion team in the 1995–96 season. They weren't very good at first. But eventually they added their names to an exclusive list. They became NBA champions.

Vince Carter was one of Toronto's first superstars. The high-flying guard arrived in 1998. He was known as a ferocious dunker. He even won the NBA All-Star Slam Dunk Contest in 2000. That summer he went viral with a

DAVIS
33
Budweiser
TORONTO
33
HEAT
6

massive dunk at the Olympics. Carter's fame helped put the Raptors on the map.

But Carter was much more than just a dunker. He finished in the NBA's top 10 in scoring four times in his six full seasons with Toronto. In 2000–01 he averaged a career-high 27.6 points per game.

After four seasons, the Raptors had yet to make the playoffs. So in 1999 they traded for veteran center **Antonio Davis**. He was a proven winner who had helped the Pacers make a number of deep playoff runs. In his first season with the Raptors, Davis helped them reach the playoffs for the first time.

STAT SPOTLIGHT

CAREER POINTS PER GAME

RAPTORS TEAM RECORD

Vince Carter: 23.4

The next season, Davis averaged a double-double. He also started for the Eastern Conference in the All-Star Game. That year, the Raptors won their first playoff series. Then they lost by just one point to the 76ers in Game 7 of the conference semifinals.

Swingman **Morris Peterson** arrived via the 2000 draft. He made the NBA All-Rookie team that year. Peterson was an excellent three-point shooter. His smooth left-handed jump shot made him a steady presence in the Raptors' lineup for seven years.

ALL-TIME GREAT

The Raptors handed their head coaching duties to **Lenny Wilkens** in 2000-01. Wilkens was at the tail end of an amazing coaching career. He won 1,332 games over 32 seasons with six franchises. That was an NBA record when he retired in 2005.

PETERSON
24
RAPTORS
24
LAKERS
8

BOSH
4
4

CHAPTER 2

BRIDGE YEARS

The Raptors won their division in 2006–07. The biggest star on that team was center **Chris Bosh**. He arrived in Toronto as a teenager in 2003. It didn't take Bosh long to blossom into an All-Star.

A remarkably consistent scorer, Bosh averaged between 22.3 and 24.0 points per game for five straight seasons. He also posted double figures in rebounds in three of his seven seasons as a Raptor. Long and lean, Bosh was too quick for most centers to guard effectively.

And he used those long arms to average more than one blocked shot per game.

Bosh left in the summer of 2010 to join LeBron James and Dwyane Wade in Miami. But the Raptors got a first-round draft pick in return. They used that pick on center **Jonas Valančiūnas** from Lithuania. Valančiūnas became a strong inside scorer and rebounder. He was also a favorite of Raptors fans, who hated to see him traded to Memphis in 2019.

DeMar DeRozan was another fan favorite. The shooting guard spent nine seasons in Toronto and was a four-time All-Star. DeRozan still holds many Raptors career

STAT SPOTLIGHT

CAREER REBOUNDS PER GAME

RAPTORS TEAM RECORD

Chris Bosh: 9.4

DeROZAN
10
VALANČIŪNAS
17

CALDERÓN
8

records, including most games played and points scored.

Point guard **José Calderón** ran the show in Toronto for seven and a half seasons. A native of Spain, Calderón thrived both as a starter and coming off the bench. From 2007–08 to 2011–12 he averaged 11.0 points and 8.1 assists per game. Calderón was an excellent free-throw shooter as well. In 2008–09 his .981 free-throw percentage led the NBA. Through 2019, Calderón was the Raptors' all-time leader with 3,770 career assists.

FILLING IT UP

DeRozan averaged more than 20 points per game in each of his last five seasons with Toronto. In 2016–17 he posted a career-high 27.3 points per game. That was fifth best in the NBA that season.

LEONARD
2

CHAPTER 3
CHAMPIONS

The 2018–19 season is one that Raptors fans will never forget. The team had won four playoff series over the previous three seasons. The Raptors were close to breaking through. Then a key trade helped put them over the top.

Toronto acquired forward **Kawhi Leonard** in a trade with San Antonio. It hurt to give up DeRozan in the deal, but Leonard delivered. He led the Raptors in scoring at 26.6 points per game. Then he increased that number to 30.5 in the playoffs. And he hit a number of huge shots along the way.

Leonard has always been known as a clutch player. His biggest shot came in Game 7 of the conference semifinals. His last-second shot from the corner bounced on the rim and dropped through the hoop to beat the 76ers and win the series. From there, Leonard and the Raptors beat the Bucks and Warriors to win their first NBA title.

Leonard left Toronto as a free agent after just one season. But point guard **Kyle Lowry** was still around to lead the way. He was a key player in the Raptors' championship season, his seventh in Toronto. Lowry averaged a

STAT SPOTLIGHT

SINGLE-SEASON THREE-POINTERS

RAPTORS TEAM RECORD

Kyle Lowry: 238 (2017-18)

LOWRY
7
RAPTORS
7
Sun Life

SIAKAM
43
RAPTORS
43

career-best 8.7 assists per game. That was second-best in the NBA.

Many of Lowry's assists went to power forward **Pascal Siakam**. In just his third year in the NBA, Siakam was the breakout star of the champion Raptors. He more than doubled his scoring average to 16.9 points per game. He also increased his rebound total to 6.9 per game. And in the playoffs, he was even better. Siakam scored 32 points in Game 1 of the NBA Finals as the Raptors beat the Warriors. Then he chipped in 26 points as Toronto clinched the title with a Game 6 win on the road.

FIVE-TIMERS CLUB

Kyle Lowry made his fifth All-Star Game appearance in 2019. That tied him with Vince Carter and Chris Bosh for the most All-Star seasons in Raptors history.

TIMELINE

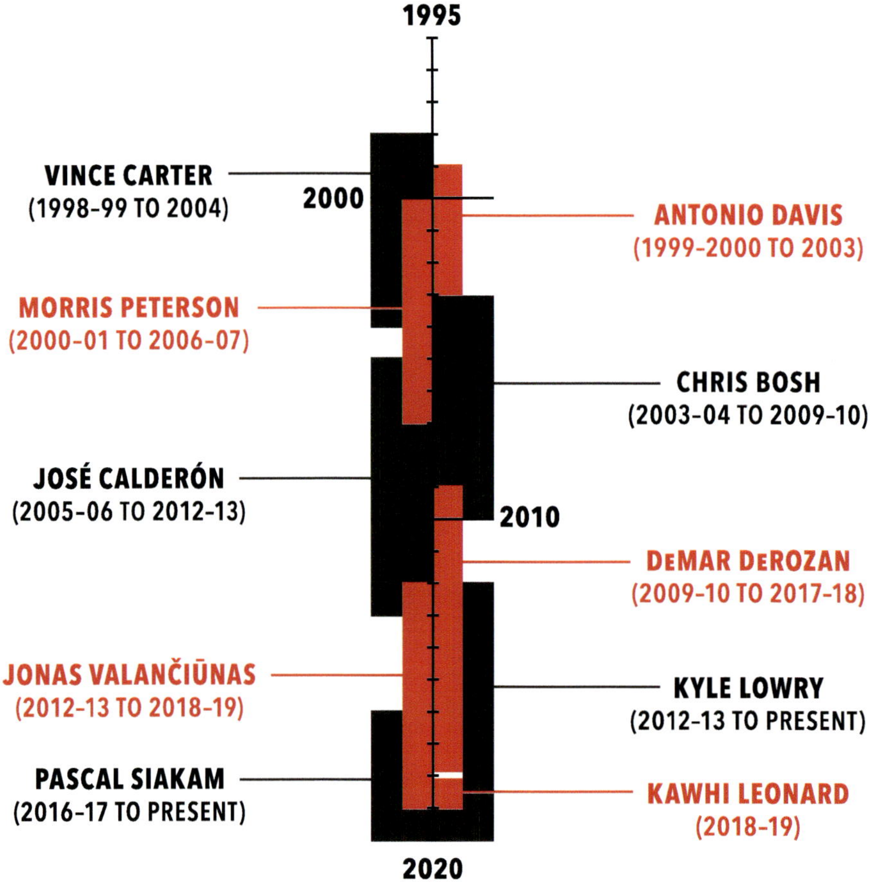
1995
VINCE CARTER
(1998-99 TO 2004)
2000
ANTONIO DAVIS
(1999-2000 TO 2003)
MORRIS PETERSON
(2000-01 TO 2006-07)
CHRIS BOSH
(2003-04 TO 2009-10)
JOSÉ CALDERÓN
(2005-06 TO 2012-13)
2010
DEMAR DEROZAN
(2009-10 TO 2017-18)
JONAS VALANČIŪNAS
(2012-13 TO 2018-19)
KYLE LOWRY
(2012-13 TO PRESENT)
PASCAL SIAKAM
(2016-17 TO PRESENT)
KAWHI LEONARD
(2018-19)
2020

TEAM FACTS

TORONTO RAPTORS

First season: 1995–96

NBA championships: 1*

Key coaches:

Dwane Casey (2011–12 to 2017–18)

320–238, 21–30 playoffs

Sam Mitchell (2004–05 to 2008)

156–189, 3–8 playoffs

Nick Nurse (2018–19 to present)

58–24, 16–8 playoffs, 1 NBA title

MORE INFORMATION

To learn more about the Toronto Raptors, go to **pressboxbooks.com/AllAccess**.

These links are routinely monitored and updated to provide the most current information available.

**Through 2018–19 season*

GLOSSARY

clutch
Able to come through in important or pressure-packed situations.

double-double
Accumulating 10 or more of two certain statistics in a game.

expansion team
A new team that is added to an existing league.

ferocious
Fierce and violent.

franchise
A sports organization.

free agent
A player whose rights are not owned by any team.

rookie
A first-year player.

swingman
A player who can play both guard and forward.

thrived
Was successful.

viral
Circulated widely and rapidly on the Internet.

INDEX